"May the God of Hope fill you with all Joy and peace as you trust in him, so that you may overflow with hope by the power of the Holy Spirit."
Romans15:13

THE WAY WE GO.

Prologue

Some journeys begin as a vague idea or something that sounds appealing to eventually try. Other Journeys, such as this one, begin as a compelling need. A quest. I needed to find the stories. To ask the questions. To hear the stories. To find the people that had the stories. More than stories, I needed miracles. Do they really happen? Do I really believe they happen?? Let's ask the questions, let's ask the people. Compelled.

So I packed my hatchback, grabbed my 24 year old cat-- because she's 24. Who else takes that on? She's blind and deaf. Nobody. So she became my "flat Stanley" of sorts. I began to think of her as "flat Minnie".

Rewind, the Sunday before, my pastor had given a sermon from John....
"I AM THE WAY THE TRUTH AND THE LIFE." He focused on THE WAY we carry the truth and the life. Basically if we change

the way, we change the truth. Show me the way Lord, your way. "The Way" began to pop up in all corners of my journey so it became a mantra of sorts. THE WAY. Because I was seeking to find the Miracles of God, I decided to trust the way of God. Seemed apt.

Flat Minnie and I turned my Toyota north and started out.

THE PLAN.

1. Hang out in local coffee shops where people linger and talk.
2. Ask the Question.
3. Write the story. Boom. One and Done.

"Have you ever seen anything you would consider to be a miracle?"

AND we're off…

Journal Entry No. 1

She stood at the edge of the
River Bank. The wind picked
up and the thunder rolled
deep and proud. She glanced up. She's been trying
to do that more often. "Look up," he whispered.
The cliff above was tall and rocky but halfway up
there were pretty yellow flowers blooming through
crevices and cracks. Jesus leaned down to
whisper in her ear "You did that. You grew in the
Rocky places." She smiled "Yes." she thought
"That made sense." With a grateful heart she
turned back toward the riverbank and looked up
again. The bird above her soared. He didn't fly, he
just floated. The air currents were unusually strong
with the impending rain so the bird didn't have to
do anything but ride the invisible air. "Trust the
current. That's what I want you to do" Jesus said.
"Just ride the current. The invisible current. I've got
the weight and the Direction." With that the rain
began to fall on her upturned face.

Miracle No. 1

The family and friends gathered around the picnic table to celebrate a new beginning, a new adventure on the mission field for a beautiful young woman. The two homeless men watched from their normal spot under the tree that provided a little shade on a hot August afternoon. One of the women from the group looked up and headed their way with two plates of food. The men were grateful as she approached and they took the plates. They said thank you with their heads down and she said "No, Please come join us. Come sit at our table." The men looked up surprised but shuffled to join the friendly group under the pavilion. One of the men shared small talk and stories and was friendly. The other man sat quietly and just listened. The next day the woman who had given them food heard a knock at her door. She lived across the street from the park but was surprised when she opened the door to the homeless man that had been so quiet the day before. He looked at her and began nervously. "I just wanted to say Thank you." he said. "I wanted to say thank you for seeing us and thank you for bringing us food and thank you for letting us join you. I have spent most of my life in prison and had forgotten what it was like to be accepted. Many church groups and families come to this park but you are the only one who has ever asked us to join you. I just wanted you to know how important and special you made me feel. It has been many years since I have felt seen."

JESUS SEES YOU.
The miracle of being included. The miracle of being seen.

There is a seat at the table for all . All means all. All means you. The table is long and welcoming. It is full of the very best things. Pull up a chair. You are invited.

Miracle No. 2

I chatted with a man and a woman within view of the Missouri River. Brick streets, old buildings, river flowing and the history of the small town hung in the air. It was dusk on a lazy beautiful summer evening. I had stopped two people leaving the cafe at the same moment that I was. I asked my question. "Have you ever had anything happen that you would consider a miracle?" The man said "Miracles are all about timing". He began to tell his story of sitting at a traffic light a few seconds too long. As he remained at the light a breadth of a second too long, a large truck barreled through the intersection directly across his path. If he had moved a moment earlier, he would have been completely blindsided. Miracle? He thought so. The friend that stood with us as we chatted joined in with the memory of a time when she had been traveling across country and pulled over to feed an infant. This stop delayed her about 45 minutes behind the cars that she had been traveling with. Just a short time later those very cars were part of a devastating pile-up that killed 60 people. The man interrupted with the quote "There but for the

grace of God go .I"   Yes sir, I believe so. The river
rolled on and so did I.

Journal Entry No. 2

After I loaded up the next morning just a few miles out of town there was a sign for a place called Backwater. It caught my eye so I wandered off of the main road down a curvy, two lane side road to nowhere. A little while later I pulled into a tiny town, an almost empty town. This town must have been a large railway station at one time. It was a historical landmark but the only thing left today was a few small stores and scattered cars. There probably weren't many people around that knew the history and significance of this town but the people that lived here did. This was the beginning of the process I began of encountering the past as I went forward in the present. The only place that even looked open was a tiny cafe. I went in and all eyes swung toward the door as I opened it. Exposed brick walls and lighting that hadn't been done on purpose and one smiling waitress greeted me. As I waited for my fries and side salad, I looked around. I did not find anybody that would even lift their eyes to meet mine. No discussion was going to happen here. "She's the reason you're here" God said almost before the question formed in my mind. My eyes landed on the waitress. He told me to leave her some money. I quietly slipped her some and I left with a "God bless". I still don't know any more details to that stop. I believe it was on purpose and I believe that God did what he wanted done. I have been learning in my life that we often

don't see the outcomes. He just wants us to believe in them. I hope that the money for her was a miracle that day. I hope it did something that needed to be done. Past that, I will pray that God multiplies it for her and for me as well. Fishes and loaves sort of thing,..

Miracle No. 3

God moves provision from hand to hand. A single mother of four was struggling to make it on her own without a car and without a job. A Jesus loving couple loaned her their van for as long as she needed to get on her feet. She worked, she saved and she began to carve out a life for herself and her children. She was able to finally buy a vehicle. Her sister was in a desperate situation and the mother of four was hoping to pass the couple's van on for her sister to borrow temporarily as well. The couple said "yes" but wanted to go a step further and give that mother the blessing of the ability to be the actual gift giver. They gave her the title and ownership of their van to pay forward. What a beautiful picture of empowering, encouraging and intentional generosity! That very day when the man of the couple came home to his wife, he was grinning from ear to ear. He had just come from the house of another elderly friend that they had been helping to care for. She had just received the news that she could no longer drive on her own. She had gifted the couple with the van she could no longer use! Jesus multiplies what we give! You cannot out give God! With open hands to give and receive, God can provide in miraculous ways!

Miracle No. 4

Music blaring, window down, a few minutes late as usual and she was headed to a Ministry meeting. It was the first Ministry meeting of this particular event. The event was to be in Montana but the process and prayer began in Missouri. As she pulled off of the highway onto a main thoroughfare, there was a man standing by the side of the road holding a sign for help. She tried to look away but the Lord tapped her on the shoulder. She reminded herself that she did ask the Lord to highlight people that He wanted her to help. He was absolutely highlighting this man. She looked in her purse to give him something. She had A $5.00 bill and a $20.00 bill. She reached for the $5.00. Jesus said "Give him the $20.00". "$20.00" she thought? That's quite a bit of money but sticking her hand out the window, she motioned to the man. As he started toward the car, he paused halfway across 4 lanes of traffic and yelled "Is that a twenty?!" in a loud excited voice. Nodding and embarrassed she gave him the money quickly. He reached into his back pocket and pulled out a plastic card and loudly announced "This goes to the first person that gives out a $20.00 bill." He announced this as if it was a game show or something. "It's for free donuts." he said as the light changed and she pulled away with the small gift card in hand. When she got to her meeting, she realized it was for a dozen free donuts every month for a year. She figured up the total amount of donuts that the card would provide and the total was $110.00. She took her daughters the next week to see if the card would work and it did! She laughed and told everybody that she had actually made money on the deal. The story became a testimony at the event in Montana and she still tells it to anyone that will listen. God multiplies what you give him to use!

Journal Entry No. 3

The struggle. When you're on a journey like this, one where the whole point is to meet and talk to strangers, you're obviously expecting to encounter some resistance and rejection. I was not prepared, however, for the total sum zero that I received. Don't get me wrong, I was having a great time. I made myself stop at anything that caught my fancy along the way. Flat Minnie required frequent stops anyway. So we stopped at RV parks, rest stops, gas stations and pretty much anywhere that claimed they had the best homemade pie along the way. Coconut cream is always worth checking out. I'd always wanted to take a cheeseburger road trip so I stopped for as many as possible. All was truly wonderful but every time I found a person to ask my question to, I was met with quizzical looks, snorts and long pauses. One lady snapped her pocketbook shut and said she had never seen anything even resembling a miracle in her whole life and stomped off! It was like cold water hitting my face. Later I decided I was truly sad for her. Hoping that my question alone would open some part of her mind that would allow her to reexamine her perspective, I moved on. Quickly. Leaving Topeka in my rearview, I wondered If a person who didn't even believe that miracles were possible had any Hope? Or had any Faith? And how do you live without hope or faith? All good contemplating material but as I continued encountering only moderate success I found myself on the floor of a hotel room in Kansas pretty discouraged.

Flat Minnie was just happy to be out of the car and made herself comfortable in the hotel sink! I questioned everything that night. I was supposed to write a book?! Crazy. I was supposed to be on this trip? Crazy. There was stuff to take care of at home. Stuff to fix. Did God even DO miracles? Where are you, Lord? I need confirmation. I need to hear. I need to know I'm not alone.

 "He's not trying to hide. Ask him, He will answer." That's what I've always told my kids. He did. Her name is Marsha.

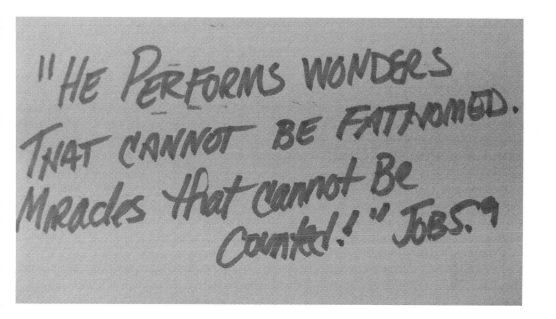

"HE PERFORMS WONDERS THAT CANNOT BE FATHOMED. Miracles that cannot Be Counted!" JOBS.9

My Miracle. Meeting Marsha. My own Miracles.
This was part of the journey. AS my jouney
continued, I was finding that my journey was
becoming my own miracle.
Most of them seem small but God intervening is
never small. However, that night I was at a low
spot. I kept rolling over and waking to questions,
heaviness, disappointment and frustration? I had
not seen or heard the things the God had said I
would. I began to think that the journey was
pointless. That I had somehow misunderstood.

Miracle No. 4

Upon waking up, I considered several things that I needed to get done. I eventually decided to go on down for breakfast but I didn't brush my teeth or put on makeup completely convinced that I would never meet any people. This was a small act of rebellion on my part. I'm sure God was smiling at the time. I grabbed coffee and a couple of plates of food. (I don't eat breakfast so this was another small act of rebellion.) I opened my Bible to no place in particular. I was looking for answers, looking for God to speak. About that time I heard a woman talking on her phone. She was accepting birthday wishes obviously from someone at home. I was surprised when she leaned in and said "What are you reading?" Because I couldn't really explain that I was just looking for some sort of hope in Jesus.   (That seemed a little dramatic.) I mumbled something appropriate. She sat down with her husband at the table next to me and began to eat. The Holy Spirit kept poking me and I finally leaned over to ask my question. "So I'm wondering if I could ask you a question. Has there ever been anything in your life that you have experienced that you would call a Miracle?" It sounds like a simple question but it is obviously not. She hesitated and my heart sank. She must have seen it on my face because she kind of smiled and shook her head said "No, no. I'm just trying to decide which one to share with you. I have seen so many!" I quickly said "I want to hear them all!" and I pulled my chair closer to her table. She introduced her husband and we began a conversation that lasted a full, fast 2 hours. We talked long past when they closed down breakfast and swept up the room. To say that it was a divine appointment is an understatement. As if that could possibly be an understatement. To me it was like the heavens parted and God answered all of my concerns, all of my fears, all of my questions in one moment. Of course he does miracles. Of course he sent me to a person that had seen so many. A person that didn't question at all. A person that knew faith was a key. I had so much to learn from her. She was from the state of Washington and it was her 50th birthday. She and her husband were on a birthday trip for her when the snow and storms had rerouted them and they ended up in Kansas. Coincidence? I think not.

Life Is A Miracle
Breath Is A Miracle
Love Is A Miracle
Sunset Is A Miracle
Babies Are A Miracle
Forgiveness Is A Miracle
Celebration Is A Miracle
Music Is A Miracle.....

Journal Entry 4

First day in Kansas I spotted an RV park. Not sure why it looked interesting but I pulled in. I found a great spot under the trees. A woman almost approached me and I waited. She opted out and moved on. Too many moments are missed. She missed the invitation. The invitation to talk miracles, hear miracles, see bigger. So I just decided to take it in. Last year the Lord told me to "Speak the beauty you see." and now I'm writing it. This spot under the trees. Sunshine beaming and sparkling. The pond is beautiful in the middle of this place. There is oppression here but there is beauty too. I realize that some of the people here are just surviving and some of the people are traveling through on their own adventure and journey. Some are permanent residents, some are pausing here. Life, right? This is perspective. Perspective in both mental and physical space. There are prisons that aren't really prisons .There is bondage that isn't really bondage. "I offer freedom to anyone." J.C.

Minnie walks around and picks a spot in the grass to bask in the sun while I breathe in deeply of fresh air, new mercies and a wish that I could pass on what I feel, what I know to be true. Hope is never lost, your situation is only as real as your ability to see that Jesus can change everything, heal anything. I pray for this park and these people. That God will move and reveal himself to them. I pray that he will bring life and hope and the ability to see the beauty, to feel the freedom. In a moment. Don't miss the moments. God moves in moments. May we have the perception to perceive them and the courage to grasp them. I leave a blessing, a person of peace. I move on. Thank you for the moment of beauty.

God moves in the moments. The beauty of timing. Movement in the moment.

Miracle No. 5

His teenage daughter was hooked up to machines and being kept alive at the hospital. There had been a tragic automobile accident. He believed in God. He believed in prayer. He believed in healing. He asked a couple of people to come pray for her, to fight for her life beside him. He believed that God wanted to and was able to heal his daughter. Even though the hospital had said there was no hope, the father called in a prayer team. That act of faith and belief alone was remarkable. In the face of a healthcare team that said there was absolutely nothing that could be done, he had enough hope to ask. The father, not wanting any doubt to weaken his faith, asked any friends and family to leave that could not and would not confess to complete confidence in his daughter's healing. Many left. So they prayed. He believed. Several days went by and there was no change. She was still unresponsive. She was still living through machines and the professionals were still saying there was no hope. They transferred her to a hospital in another city that was supposed to be more specialized. When they arrived at the new hospital they were once again told that there was no hope. The father boldly announced "I will not accept that. I accept and stand on the belief that God will save her. God has the last word, not man." He was right. God did have the last word and that man's daughter later walked out of that hospital whole and healed. That father believes in the miraculous .He took actions to step out in his belief. Sometimes the hardest part is believing enough to ask.

"With God all things are possible." ASK.

YOUR WORDS
CREATE

CULTURE.

Prov. 18:21

Miracle No. 6

She directed a healing room. She believed in healing, had seen God heal. So when she was asked to be prayer support for a local church, she agreed without hesitation. It was a Catholic Church run by a Catholic priest that was spirit-filled. This speaks of a church that was functioning in spiritual gifts, believing for healing and asking for the impossible. So she went to pray. While she was there she encountered a young man that could only hear out of one of his ears and his speech was the product of that limited hearing. He came forward to ask for prayer. He asked them to pray that he would be able to hear. She prayed for him and then asked him if he could hear any sounds. The answer was "no". It was the same, no change. Not dissuaded and believing that God wanted hearing for this young man, she prayed again. As she persisted in that prayer, the young man felt something in his ear and it opened up and he could immediately hear. At the same time he began to speak without the speech impediment that he had always had. He was overjoyed and grateful to God.

He and the woman became good friends. A few years later she was in his wedding and still carries a picture of them around today. A testimony to what God does and wants to do through people who are willing to believe and to ASK.

Journal Entry No. 5

Still on the Way.....

I saw a Church on the highway today. I was compelled to check it out. The only outstanding thing was a huge sign outside the front "I am the way, I am the truth and the life. No man comes to the father but by me." The way. Hmmmm... Reminds me of Josh's sermon the Sunday before I left. The way we do the truth and the way we do the life is just as important as the truth and the life. If we change the way, we change the truth and we change the life. Jesus is the way. The only way. The only truth. The only life. And Jesus does his way with love. Always.

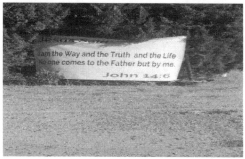

Miracle No. 7

Standing on the steps of the Little White Church my great grandfather pastored in Lucas Kansas, I felt the weight of that Heritage settle on me. Weird but

true. Lucas is one of the most beautiful places I've ever seen. Wilson Lake and the surrounding area is rolling hills, big open skies, remnants of stone fences and sparkling waters. As I drove past the lake and through the hills on the way into town, I just said "Lord, I feel you here." in an off handed manner. I was a little surprised when he answered. "Yes, I walk these hills." I paused and laughed. "Yes, yes, of course you do...who wouldn't?" There was so much art, history and beauty around Lucas. This was the beginning of a journey within a journey for me. I began to understand spiritual inheritance. Stake your land, fight for your heritage. Jesus paid already. God wants us to access all that is ours in Him. We have an inheritance. Ask him what yours is. He will show you.

Miracle No. 8

There was a precious couple I met in the middle of the street in a little town called Lucas Kansas. She was from England originally and had an English accent and he was a gentle soft-spoken man that had retired from engineering and then gotten his PhD in counseling. They traveled one summer to walk the El Camino in Spain. (Side note: when I started writing this story out and went to google this trip, I realized that this meant "THE WAY" in Spanish and that it was a pilgrimage. Of course it is!! God has such a sense of humor. They both said that they had seen the hand of God in a miraculous way on that trip. She said that God brought the most amazing people, the most amazing places to stay and the most amazing connections. He brought provision of every kind at every moment that they needed it. He said that as they walked along, people would walk and join them for a while. Many of them would talk with him in depth about the reason for their journey. Of course a lot of people are searching for something that is on this pilgrimage. His counseling, his listening, his wisdom, he was able to counsel and speak life. He was able to release encouragement to hurting people one after another along the way. His wife was in every way his partner with a soft smile, warm heart and gentle manner. They spoke specifically of helping people deal with feelings of unforgiveness And betrayal. I wish I had stories from the people they counseled. No doubt there was healing and freedom along those many miles together. They stayed at hostels along the way with fellow journeymen and shared a meal   and conversation in the evenings. Each of this couple said that the way the Lord connected people on that journey was miraculous. The way again. This looks like the way of Jesus to me. Does it to you? The journey, the breaking bread, the sharing? The way of Jesus? For them, each day was dedicated to a different member of their family as they walked in faith and prayed for each one of them. I have no doubt that those prayers were answered and multiplied by their obedience and love of people. Since I met this couple and heard of this journey I have met many more who took the same journey and have all had the same testimony. At night the hostels that they stay in and the breaking of bread with people from other countries and cultures, the sharing of the good news is nothing short of miraculous. I feel blessed to have learned of this and heard so many stories of it. I plan to do it myself one day.

Post Journey Discovery:

I just met a woman who was taking that same journey and recounting it on social media. It was amazing and I am including one of her excerpts straight off of social media. It is so incredible to hear and see what God does every day with people who are willing. This El Camino really peaks my interest. I believe it's in my wheelhouse.   One day in the life.

Also met a couple from Spain and Germany, a couple who we got to share with and also pray with. They have been hitchhiking prior to the Camino and I believe God used us to share the good news with these women.

John Michael has to be one of my biggest highlights of the Camino. I hardly ever meet a real Christian but today it happened. We had CHURCH at the cafe we met him at.

We even had a Bible study and some worship. As he played Lauren Dagle's 🎵 "You say." 🎵 we worshipped and he said "Where three are gathered..." and I included "God is in their midst."

He then shouted out in French "Merci Señor!!!!" as he looked up into heaven.

It was incredible 🔥

He then shouted out in French "Merci Señor!!!!" as he looked up into heaven.

It was incredible 🔥

He was a firecracker and reminded me on Clint Bokelman. We would be like "Wow, you are an amazing believer" and he would respond "It's normal."

Yep....living radically for Jesus IS normal. It's the way. The BEST.

Since leaving America, I have been able to share with 16 nations to date.

Please pray for us for more re-encounters with pilgrims. We have been building each day on relationships and building more.

Please pray for good news on good soil 🏴

Declaration

Thank you, God. Confirmation. You are so good. He does see. He does hear. He does speak. He does do Miracles. Check, check, check, check. The song "Goodness of God" by Bethel plays in my head. What is your Marsha? Who is your Marsha? Have you even asked God for a Marsha? A confirmation of his plan for you? A confirmation of his purpose in your life? Ask for a Marsha. Today.

"He performs wonders that cannot be fathomed and miracles that cannot be counted."- Job 5:9

Miracle No. 9

The young couple was invited to a healing service by a friend. Having both grown up in traditional churches they had not been exposed much to the idea of healing and believing for that. Her friend had insisted they try it. The couple had been trying, unsuccessfully, to conceive a child for quite a long time; they were feeling hopeless. That night the preacher said "Stand if you need healing for salvation, a dark Night of the soul or pornography". Both she and her husband stood. They both heard the pastor say "Everyone, please stand" so the two of them stood up but they were only a few people standing because, of course, this was not what the pastor had said. The pastor went to them and said to her "You have had a dark night of the soul." "What the heck?" she thought but kept to herself. As the pastor began to describe what he thought she had experienced, she realized and identified with a time of intense grief when her father had passed away. She had been his caretaker and deeply grieved when he was gone. The pastor prayed for her healing and then asked the women sitting behind her to put their hands on her and pray that she would have a child. The pastor had NOT been told why they were there. He then instructed her to see him at the end of the service. During the ministry time, she went forward to hear what he had to say. He told her that she would have a son within the year. The next week her fertility doctor prescribed a new drug and she thought maybe that was her new hope for conception. However the new medicine made her terribly sick. Disappointed and confused, she went back and listened to the recording of the prayer and prophetic word that she had received the night of the healing service. The pastor had said very clearly "You will not have a baby by medical means." Stepping out in faith, she discontinued the use of her medicine. The following month she was pregnant. Sure enough she gave birth to a son within the year. This began a new journey of faith and living with an expectation of the miraculous that she lives by and testifies about to this day.

Miracle No. 10

She was from England but had gotten married, come to the states and had children here. Several years into her marriage she was at a prayer group when the question of the day was "Is there a dream in your heart that has not been answered?" She tentatively spoke up when it came her turn. After she pondered the question, she said that she had always dreamed of moving back to England for a period of time. Not forever, but her parents and siblings were still there. She had given up hope that it would ever happen. The dream still lingered back and underneath something inside Her. Her husband already had a career in the states. The leader of the study encouraged her to pray about it and ask the Lord again. Not much time had passed when her husband got a call from a college in England that wanted to offer him a job. The call was out of the blue, unexpected and not even on his radar! They took the job. It turned out that she was going to be only a very short distance from her parents. She had never thought she would live close to her family again. In the few years that they were over there, her father became ill and passed away and she was there to care for her mother. She got that precious personal gift of extra irreplaceable time with her father before he died and necessary time to take care of her mother after he was gone. This was such a blessing to her heart. It was such a miracle for her and such an answer to prayer. Only God knew the desires of her heart. Is there a dream in your heart that the Lord has not answered? Perhaps it's time to ask him again.

Journal Entry No. 6

This morning started on scripture. "Lord let the morning bring me word of your unfailing love for I have put my trust in you! Show me the way I should go. For to you, I lift up my soul."
Psalms 143-8

Show me the way I should go. My Flesh may fail. My heart might feel faint, my mind might be full of confusion but I surrender. I Surrendered. No. I AM Surrendering. Always. Again. Surrendering. Surrendering my plans. Surrendering my trust. Surrendering my mistrust. Surrendering my unbelief . Surrendering myself. "I don't live for me anymore, I live for you." (2 Cor. 5:16) Forever surrendering these things and more. A deliberate choice. A deliberate act. I choose your way. Not my way.

Your way. You ARE the way.

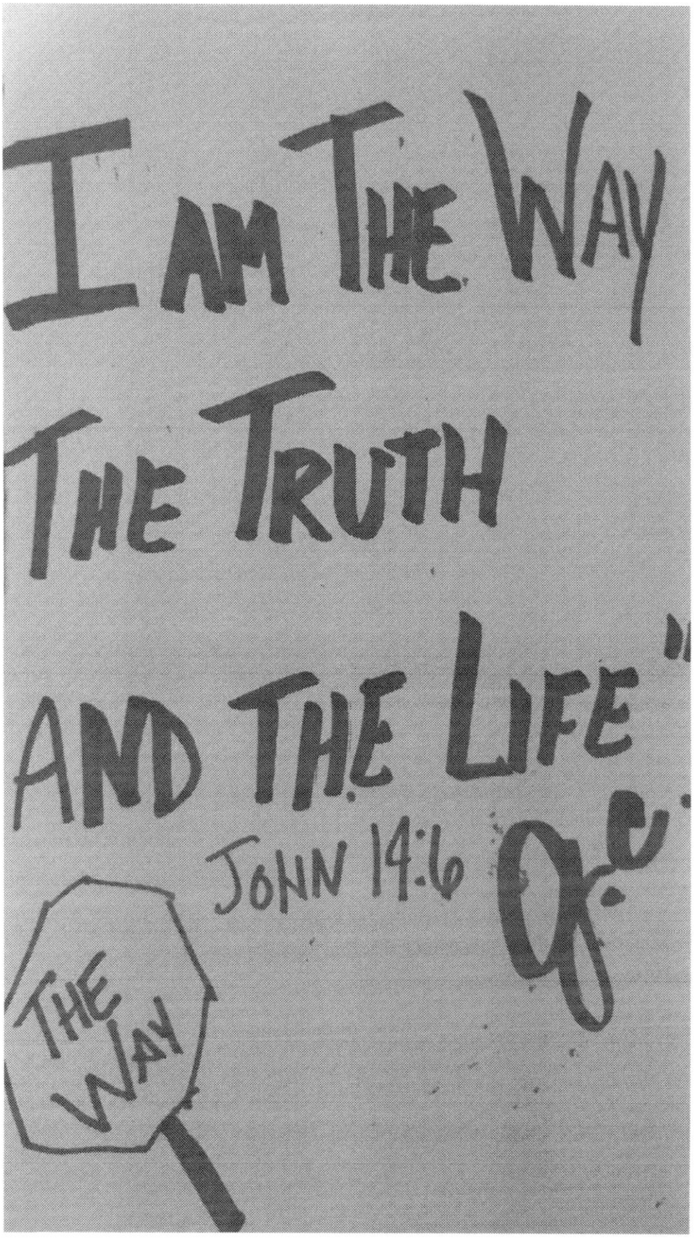
I AM THE WAY
THE TRUTH
AND THE LIFE"
JOHN 14:6
THE WAY

THE WAY

Metanarrative- the same story over and over again within a story. A repeating theme. The Bible is a meta-narrative.

Meta-miracle -- A miracle within a miracle. A repeating theme. This journey is a meta -miracle. A miracle within a miracle about miracles.
God breathed word. Crazy stuff. Crazy life. Crazy good.

Journal Entry No. 7

The way through the Mountains. The pass.
This driving through the mountains. There is an
unwinding taking place, and unwrapping, an
unveiling. And as it does, something begins to peek
out. This thing Begins to show itself by opening the
door just a crack. My breath becomes deeper and
slower. My shoulders lower. My heart releases.
What is this familiar thing? Is it you Lord? Is it me?
I recognize her. The cars race by as if oblivious to it
all. The profound shifting taking place in my soul.
"Slow down." I think "Don't miss it." Where are
they in such a hurry to? What is so pressing? Can
it not wait a moment or two? Can't they feel it too?
The drumbeat. To remember, to untangle, to
stretch and to dance? To recognize the one who
created it all? To recognize the one designer and
the designed? I can wait. I can slow. An
unbecoming? To become who I was meant to be?
To UNBECOME those things I was not meant to
be? Take a step out onto the dance floor. Totally
and completely free in you, my heart recognizes
this. My soul leaps out at this Freedom in you.

THE PASS —

BRIGHT YELLOW ASPENS —
MOUNTAIN SIDE — SPARKLING RIVER —
DEPTHS OF THE VALLEY — HEIGHT
OF THE MOUNTAINTOPS — DARK WALL
OF THE CLIFFS — BRIGHT GREEN OF
VALLEY PASTURES — SHARP ANGLES OF
ROCKS — CURVES — HILLS — TUNNEL —
SUNLIGHT — TEXTURES — COLORS —
DEPTHS — RUSHING WATER —

GOD SAID — WRITE YOUR BOOK
LIKE THIS.

" THE BRILLIANCE OF LIFE "

Journal Entry No. 8

A course. A purpose. A direction. A Calling. A fulfilling. A Heritage I can't deny. A joining, a mingling an adding. A Becoming and an Unbecoming. What does that look like? Nothing. Absolutely nothing. To you. To me it is everything.

Maybe life is not so much about becoming something but about Unbecoming all of the things we were never meant to be. Unbecoming fearful. Fear floats away and adventure takes over. Curiousness wins. I step out.   Do you need to step out?

What Do
you need
to
unBecome?

_____

_____

_____

Journal Entry No. 9

Speaking of and on perspective, I drove up on the Grand Mesa outside of Grand Junction Colorado today. The Aspen trees had turned yellow. Made me think "The hills are alive with the sound of music." You get the picture. Sunny. Hard not to see the benevolent Creator. Hard not to breathe in abundant life from that vantage point. When I was 8, I stood on that mountaintop and my Uncle Jim said "How do you suppose anyone can you look at this and not believe there is a God?" Drop the mic. Bam. There It Is. My Moment. Eyes Wide Open. Mountain top experiences. Lands' End. 11,000 foot altitude. As I drove up the mountain today remembering that moment John Denver poured through my head with "Rocky Mountain High." Absolutely. The Highest. My Soul connected with a God who brought me full circle again. His view. His perspective. Not mine. Believe in the impossible. Nothing is too big. Soul connections. **Find the place your soul connects with God and go there. Often.**

THOUGHTS?

Miracle No. 11

Her daughter attended college 8 hours away. The mother frequently prayed for safety, for friends, for health, life, protection and provision for her daughter. She was particularly diligent when the daughter was on the road traveling 8 hours each direction by herself. On the drive home for spring break the daughter was traveling through rain on a curvy area of Arkansas when her car tumbled off the road at a high rate of speed. The pavement was wet and her car flipped a couple of times. The parents got the call and headed to Arkansas but it was 5 hours away. The five hours seemed more like15 as they tried to get to their daughter. When they arrived she was safe and sound. She had been taken care of by a local fire and police department. There was not a bruise on her. Anywhere. Several people that had witnessed the wreck said that after turning over a couple of times, the car had skidded to a stop upside down on its hood. She had been hanging from her seat belt in the top of the car. She kicked the window to get out of the car. Of course there were tears and hugs and everyone was tremendously grateful. She knew that her grandparents prayed daily for her protection and she knew that her mother and father prayed for her protection as well. It seemed obvious that the Lord had protected her on the trip. The daughter testified that she knew God was protecting her as the car spun out of control because it was if God was saying. "No matter what is spinning around you, you are still and at peace". The mother laid in bed the following morning thanking Jesus privately and silently when she heard in her head so very clearly the voice of God. "See, I told you I had her." She crawled out of the bed, walked into the kitchen and knelt to lay face down on the floor. She could do nothing but praise the Lord for the sound of his voice and for the obvious answer to her prayers. The confirmation that God had purposely and intentionally protected her daughter began to grow the faith of a small David facing a huge Goliath. God is bigger. Always.

Miracle No. 12

She and a friend were so excited because they were headed to a town just a few minutes away and they we're going to get to hear Bill Johnson speak and preach. She casually remarked along the way that she would love to have her hearing ability prayed for. When they got there the place was full and a couple other people that they knew called them over with open seats. At the end of the service Bill Johnson was asking about different things that people needed prayer for. When he asked if anyone there had hearing loss and needed prayer, A few people raised their hands so she raised hers. She had an 80% hearing loss in her left ear. It was significant enough that she could not talk on the phone with that ear because she was unable to hear what was said. Bill Johnson asked the people around her to put their hands on her and pray for healing in her ear. She said it felt like a lightning bolt just started through her ear and it just sort of popped and opened up. She received complete and total hearing in that instant and still has it to this day. Instant healing. Some say it doesn't happen. If you had been healed you would disagree.

Miracle No. 13

Her son began to show signs of autism at 18 months. She was a believer in spiritual gifts and she had gotten a prophetic word when he was born that he would be an incredible musician. The struggles he was having made it look like that would not be possible. Believing that what she was seeing was not the whole story or the whole truth, she began to search for answers. By faith, she started a journey of therapies, diet changes, research and prayer. She persevered and believed for 7 years. At 8 years old he was a totally normal child. Hope makes a difference. Belief in the impossible makes a difference. Today he plays in an orchestra in Kansas City Missouri and has a very successful career. She chose to believe what had been spoken by God and kept pressing in and pressing on. She was confident that someday he would be the person and musician that she had been told he would be. Most people would say that autism is not curable. All things are possible for those who believe! You are who God says you are.

Miracle No. 14

She took the tour through this beautiful campus in California. Her young, excited heart burst at the possibilities of a life here, a beginning here. She so desperately wanted to attend this private school but financially it was impossible. Her mother had said they could check it out. They went together as a family. They all fell in love with the school. It was such a perfect fit for the daughter. This instantly became a dream for all of them. They were at lunch excitedly discussing the tour they had just been on when the mother bodily proclaimed "God Will Make A Way! He will send a scholarship or a stipend or some other means. He will make the way. I believe this." Literally as she was speaking these words, the daughter received a call from the school. She was immediately offered a scholarship **AND** a stipend! The mother had seen enough provision and prayers answered in her lifetime to know the heart of God. To have experienced the extravagant nature of a God who fulfills dreams of those who love him. A God who loves to give, loves to provide and loves to bless those who love him and believe in Him. The Challenge. Can you believe this? Proclaim this? He is not a sour and stingy God. He is extravagant and rich in mercy and love and forgiveness. He wants to show you this. Challenge, ask, proclaim. She proclaimed. He showed up.

Journal Entry No. 9

I went South in Eastern Colorado. Strange the difference one turn makes. I drove through miles and miles of dead and dry land. Empty land. Crying out for life and water land. Tractors left in the field land. No houses, no cars, no animals, no vegetation, no people, no barns, no telephone lines. Literally there were no signs of life for a very long time. No Rivers of Life here. I drove through a place that used to be called Horsecreek but only a couple of horses could be spotted on thousands of acres. Sugar Creek used to be a thriving town of commerce and growth. In its place is a crumbling plantation and a poverty filled stop on the road that doesn't even offer a gas station. You see, I was literally looking for a bottle of water for Flat Minnie. I had been looking for a place to stop for miles and turned the wrong way. Such a stark reminder of how important a turn in direction is. I had to turn and go back the way I came. There were only dirt roads that lead to nowhere in this direction. I literally turned around and headed to water. Crowley County used to be a

booming Mecca of Orchards and ranches. Without water everything dies. The lesson here? Water brings life. Find the River. Tap into it, protect it and grow. Don't sell it off, don't trade it off, don't underestimate it. Your ability to get to the water keeps you alive. Your soul is the same. Only Living water brings life.

"We come alive in the River." (Jesus Culture I believe) Check that song out. Rivers of Life. That's what Jesus promises.

Yeah....strange the difference one turn makes. Turned out the other direction was water, life, history and community.

"If anyone is thirsty let him come to me and drink. Whoever believes in me, as the scripture has said, streams of living water will flow from within him."

John 7:37

Miracle No. 15

At 25 she began to have an extremely sharp pain in her upper left cheek. She described it as a lightning bolt of excruciating pain. It began to happen every day for a few seconds at a time and then over time more often and longer periods. Her face would seize up and her eye would close and her face would swell. She had to give up her job as an engineer. For six years this continued to get worse. She said that her life became darker and darker. Their home became darker and darker. When a light bulb went out they wouldn't replace it because light hurt her eyes. Not just physically did their life become darker, but emotionally as well. After six years the doctors diagnosed her with an incurable pain condition called TN. For the next 9 years they continued to treat her with medicines, injections and surgeries. All of these only brought temporary relief. This disease is nicknamed the suicide disease because people that have it literally cannot get away from the pain. They wind up taking their own lives in desperation. Nine more years she suffered and cried out to the Lord that she could not endure on her own any longer. He would have to help her if she were to live with this. She was at the end of her rope. They had prayed for everything. They prayed for good doctors, they had prayed for lessened pain, they prayed for medicine that would work, they had prayed for everything except that it would be taken away. There was a local pastor who had a guest speaker coming that had been healed from cerebral palsy. Her husband insisted they go. At the end of the service the pastor announced that this woman would pray for anyone that wanted prayer. The woman with TN was ready to leave but her husband implored her to stay and receive prayer. She went to the woman praying and said "I don't really believe in this healing thing." The lady that had been healed from cerebral palsy said "That's okay. I can believe enough for both of us." That woman asked if she could touch her face as she prayed. Nobody ever touched her face because it was so sensitive but she agreed. The woman said a simple prayer and then the couple said "Thank you" and left for home. Our friend that was suffering did not mention that the back of her neck began to feel warm as the woman touched her and prayed. All the way home she felt a tingling spread from the back across the whole left side of her face. This went on for 25 minutes and then she said she felt nothing. There was no pain, there was nothing. When telling the story, she said that it was crazy because it wasn't like she had great faith or like she was super spiritual. God just loved her. It had nothing to do with anything she had done or accomplished. They were so impacted that they sold their house and all of their belongings and went to be missionaries. They tell people how much Jesus loves them. She said they can't believe that they are lucky enough to live the beautiful life that they have. God loves them but he loves you too! He loves you enough. I promise. Ask him to show you how much!

THE WIND UP

So much is Miraculous
When I shifted my focus —
Journey to find miracles —
Saw then Everywhere!

What are You looking for?

Journal Entry No. 10

"Where does this journey end?" I asked.

"Freedom," J.C. said "This is what life with me was intended to look like. Listen to me; walk with me. I will provide for you. Live through me. There's total freedom in that." The miraculous happens every day. You have to be open to it. You have to be willing to see it. Just ask for it today. Ask the Lord to show you the miraculous in your life.

Is it ordinary or extraordinary? Could it be that the extraordinary IS the ordinary?

"I will not allow my miracle to be trapped in my mundane." Stephen Furtick (I just heard this in one of his sermons!)

Jesus invites us. He calls us. He calls you. Do you hear it?   Lean in. Can you hear the drumbeat? I so do.

I CHALLENGE YOU TO PICK A SEAT AT THE TABLE, ask Jesus to SHOW YOU THE MIRACLES!

 In fact, I dare you to ask him for the extraordinary. I pray that he shows you the extravagance of his love for you. Eph. 3:20

LIFE IS FAR TOO SHORT TO MISS THE LAVISHNESS OF GOD.

Miracle No. 16

I met a lady who loves the Lord but before she came to love the Lord she said that her family was far from God. Her sister and her brother-in-law were at one time severe alcoholics in South Dakota. They owned and ran a little gas station and mini mart. They turned part of the mini mart into a little bar. There was a Christian man that lived not too far away and his practice was to ask the Lord what he was to do every morning. So one particular morning he woke up and asked the Lord "What are we going to do today? Where would you have me go?" and the Lord told him to go to this little gas station / bar and talk to the owner and tell him about Jesus. He did this. That owner was my friend's brother in law. He was nice to the man but not at all interested in Jesus. He sent him on his way after giving him a free tank of gas. The next morning the Christian man asked the Lord "What would you have me do today? Where would you have me go?" The Lord told him to go again to the little gas station/ bar and to tell the man about Jesus. So he did this. My friend's brother in law again was nice and sent him home with a bag of groceries but wasn't interested in Jesus. The third morning in a row the man woke up and asked the Lord "What should we do today? Where would you have me go?" And the Lord said "I want you to go to that gas station / bar and tell the man about Jesus." The man obeyed. He went back to the bar and he talked the man again about Jesus. That was the miracle day. On that day her brother in law was open and received Jesus. He immediately was delivered from alcohol and had a radical life transformation. He put as much passion into telling people about Jesus as he had done into his drinking. He began a Thursday night bible study and worship for other men that he knew. My friend's sister was still drinking and not interested in things of God at all. For a few months, my friend's brother in law prayed and waited. One particular Thursday night she was out with her friends and just felt compelled to stop drinking early and go back to her house. The men's Bible study was in full swing. They were actually right in the middle of praying for her. When she got home she walked through the kitchen and started to go into the living room. At the threshold of the living room, she fell out face down onto the floor. She was out in the spirit for 2 hours and woke up completely transformed!   To this day they are both strong believers and Jesus followers. After that, my friend became a Believer as well. This literally changed the course of their family, their heritage and history because the one man was obedient and asked the Lord what he should do every the morning. If we all got up and asked the Lord what we should do today I wonder what would happen.

Thoughts? Examples? Experiments?

Miracle No. 17

The couple headed out on their trip across the country. They had many things to accomplish but along the way they would stop and visit with people. They would stop and show people how much Jesus loved them. Their goal was to be a blessing to others. Always. They did this in any way that they could. Their goal was to carry the Holy Spirit and deposit that Spirit wherever they went. They had been given a gift card with $100 worth of gasoline on it. That is what they intended to use to finance the travel. As they went, there were storms and weather issues that changed their path several times and extended their trip. As they went, they prayed for the cities and states they went through. They prayed for the people that they met. They didn't rush through places but extended their time and patience where love was needed. The husband fixed things that needed fixing at restaurants and places along the way. The wife chatted with other women and delivered encouragement wherever she could. I suspect they traveled much like Jesus did. The spirit and priority of the day was the people that they came in contact with rather than the list of things to accomplish and destinations to get to. After a couple of weeks and what they figured to be $200. or $300. worth of gasoline, they made it back home. The miracle of the day was that their gasoline card had never run out. They had continued to use the $100 gift card for the whole trip. Be obedient to God's agenda and he provides. The man with cattle on a thousand hills and all of the land that the cattle graze on is no more worried about money and providing for you than he is about the sun coming up in the morning or the birds being fed or the flowers being dressed.

_____

_____

_____

Journal Entry No. 11
The MIRACLE journey

What is your journey? When is your journey?
The Journey that Claims your soul?

What turns you inside out?

Do you remember?

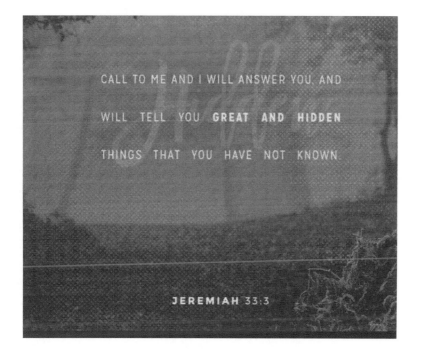

CALL TO ME AND I WILL ANSWER YOU, AND
WILL TELL YOU **GREAT AND HIDDEN**
THINGS THAT YOU HAVE NOT KNOWN.

JEREMIAH 33:3

Miracle No. 18

She was in her senior year of nursing school. Her back pain began in the fall and continued until the spring. The pain became continually worse. She believed in God and healing so she asked for healing consistently through the months. The doctor diagnosed her with sciatic nerve pain resulting from so much sitting in class and hours of studying. They told her to take ibuprofen and it would eventually get better. Eventually It got so bad that she attended a new event at her local church called "Friday night Fire". That night a young man gave his testimony and then asked if there were people in the audience who had lower back pain. He asked them to come forward for prayer. She went forward to be prayed over. The young man prayed for healing but he also got a word of knowledge for her and told her that he kept hearing the word "unforgiveness". She laughed when she told me the story because she said that she did not receive the word from him because it hurt her pride. She had been asking God for healing for months and surely if she had unforgiveness in her heart, he would have shown her that. She said that it shook her up because it didn't sound like the God that she knew to punish her with back pain for unforgiveness that she didn't realize she had. She didn't tell anyone of the word she received wrote it down and asked God to bring it back around if it was correct. She went on with her life and her chronic pain. Her pain became so bad that she would carry pillows with her if she had to sit in a hard chair for too long and she was only 22 years old. Her parents insisted a short time later that she get an MRI. She said she was actually hoping that the MRI would find something so that they would know how to fix it. However, the test came back completely clean and showed that nothing was wrong. As she was in the grocery store with a friend and complaining about the fact that the test showed nothing wrong and yet she continued to suffer, her friend stopped and looked at her with a funny look. Her friend said " I have not been wanting to ask you this but every time I pray for you the Lord tells me to ask you if you have any unforgiveness." The girl I was speaking with said she just fell out laughing in the middle of the grocery store aisle. Clearly that was the issue.

She had not told anyone of the word unforgiveness that the young man had given her at Friday Night Fire. It was Easter break and both of her roommates were gone. She woke up trying to decide what to do one day when the Lord gently prompted her to spend some time on what he had suggested. So she said she sat down with her Bible and a notebook and expected it to be about a five-minute ordeal. She said that she genuinely did not know who she had not forgiven so God could just tell her and she would repent and be done. The Lord began to reveal people to her one by one who had hurt her and that she had tucked bad feelings for in her heart. The first person was an old basketball Coach. She started answering questions that the Lord laid out before her as person after person came to her mind. Three hours later she had freed herself and forgiven every name brought before her. When she had renewed a deep relationship with Jesus a couple of years before she had prayed a blanket prayer of forgiveness for everyone that had hurt her, but the Lord wanted her to go back and be more specific. Her exact words to me were "He loved me too much to just heal my back." You see, when she was done with the list, her whole left leg became really hot and heavy and she couldn't move it. She said she was literally stuck sitting on her bed for an hour that way and then the pain was gone. She said she didn't tell anyone and woke up to go to work the next morning and still no pain. A couple of days later still no pain. To this day, no pain. You see God wants to heal every part of us. Sometimes what he's looking for when we have physical pain is for us to bring it to him in order that he can heal something spiritual or emotional as well. He wants our whole bodies healed. "Here on earth as it is in heaven". He wants us and loves us too much to only heal part of us. Here are the questions that he asked her to go over for each person that he brought to mind. Perhaps you should sit down and ask these questions of the people that the Lord would bring to your mind. What if he loves you too much to leave you unhealed in parts of yourself? WHAT IF he loves you so much that he wants you whole, healed and ABUNDANT?! WHAT IF EVERY thing you have ever hoped, dreamed and longed for is wound up in loving Jesus? Loving people extravagantly? Glorious fullness, abundant life, unending joy? Too good to be true stuff?? What if you asked him for TOTAL healing? Completeness in Him? What if you let go of the unforgiveness? What if you unbecome all of the things that hold you back? Sit down with Jesus, open your soul and see what happens? Ask him what YOUR inheritance is from him? Your purpose? Your miracle?

DO You hear the drumbeat?

Can You step out ?

Her steps to forgiveness. You should try them.

1. What did that person do?
2. How did that make you feel?
3. What did it cause you to believe about yourself?
4. What did it cause you to believe about God?
5. Plead the blood of Jesus over the offense, over the wound and over that person .
6. Pray blessing and favor over that person.

I did this myself and I have to admit that I was shocked, humbled and transformed.

The going home. The journey home. The
Miraculous Journey about the miraculous Jesus.
Jesus, Home. Full circle. I am the way.

I carry this home.

New thoughts. New Freedom. New understanding.
New goals. New purpose. New breath. "I will make
all things new.'

"And he who was seated on the throne said BEHOLD, I AM MAKING ALL THINGS NEW." also he said "Write this down for these words are trustworthy and true." Revelation 21:5

"MY WORDS ARE SPIRIT AND LIFE." John 6:63

I turn the car home with Newness. He offers it to you as well. "You are the Hallelujah" he told me. You are too! He told me that as well. I can literally hear his smile.

My stories gathered and in their basket,

**Flat Minnie and I head home..
until next time,**

LET YOUR SOUL OUT TO PARTY

"I blow through the earth with power." J.C

The Merge

The journey and the story sort of meld here. Although I guess they always have. I got a call from Marsha today. New miracle story. She has a friend that is a new Christian, a young man in her church. She was having a vehicle fixed for a woman in their church and asked this young man to pick it up and take it to the shop to have the work done for this woman. There was only a particular amount of money in the budget available to have the car fixed. They were able to have several things replaced and fixed for her but were unable to replace the tires that needed replacing at this time. When the young man delivered the car to the woman, they noticed that it had a brand new set of tires on it. They were shocked! The woman thought he had put them on, he thought the shop had put them on. They continued to check with anyone who had come in contact with the car and nobody was able to explain how it happened. Marsha was excited because not only did the woman get to experience the miraculous movement of God, but it was such an exciting testimony for the young man who had actually taken the car and knew first hand that nobody else had been involved but God. God can do what he wants and he wants to move. He wants to wow us. He wants us to be bowled over by what he does for us and how much he loves us. Here. Now. Think of the good things you would like to do for your children. He wants to do the same. He wants us to know that it's Him. He wants us to ask Him. Pray Bigger. He likes Big Prayers and the faith it takes to pray them. Just like you want your kids to believe in your goodness, he wants us to believe in his.

The Wind Up

My prayer is that each page of this book has inspired text. That it would quite literally be his hand on mine, His story of His love. "His words with His blood". That each page has something miraculous on it. That the book itself is a miracle for people. That each page is something funny or enlightening or freeing. That it would Open the Eyes of people to a different face of God. That it would Shore up Faith; it would build up hope, that it would begin a chain of people believing in Miracles and asking for miracles. This is my prayer, this is my vision. In HIM is my hope.

"Not by might, not by power but by my spirit"
                                Zech.4:6

Made in the USA
Monee, IL
27 January 2020

20915878R00061